The Prayer of

rayer of Re

The Prayer of Subm

The Praye

The Prayer of Pr

sion

The Pray

The Prayer of

a gift for:

....

from:

....

STORMIE OMARTIAN

SEVEN

Prayers

THAT WILL CHANGE YOUR LIFE FOREVER

Published by J. Countryman, a division of Thomas Nelson, Inc., Nashville, Tennessee 37214.

Project manager, Terri Gibbs
Design: The DesignWorks Group, www.thedesignworksgroup.com

www.thomasnelson.com
www.jcountryman.com

ISBN: 1-4041-0361-9

Printed and bound in the United States of America

contents

The eyes of the LORD are
on the righteous,
and His ears are open
to their prayers.

— 1 PETER 3:12

The Prayer of

rayer of Re

The Prayer of Subm

The Prayer

The Prayer of Pr

The Pray

sion The Pray

The Praye

The Prayer o

salva

During the first couple of years I walked with the Lord, my prayers went something like this:

"God, help me to get that job."

"Jesus, please heal my throat."

"Lord, send enough money to pay these bills."

"Father, take away my fear."

It took me a while to realize that those spur-of-the-moment prayers were not accomplishing much. I guess I thought the idea was to do the best I could on my own, and then if I needed a lifeline from God, I grabbed for it. The only problem was I needed a lifeline every other minute.

I loved the Scripture that says, "Ask, and it will be given to you; seek, and you will find; knock, and it will be opened to you" (Matt. 7:7). I took God at His Word and was asking, seeking, and knocking on a pray-as-you-go basis. I also took to heart the Scripture that says, "You do not have because you do not ask" (James 4:2). *Great! I can easily remedy that,* I thought, and I proceeded to ask for everything. But I was still not happy, and I didn't see the kind of answered prayer I desired.

One day as I was again reading that same verse, my eyes were opened to the next verse, "You ask and do not receive, because you ask amiss, that you may spend it on your pleasures" (James 4:3). Could it be that the "God-give-me-this, do-that, wave-your-magic-wand-here, get-me-out-of-this-mess" kind of praying was not what God desired for my prayer life? In utter frustration I said, "Lord, teach me how I'm supposed to pray."

He did exactly that!

I came to understand that prayer is not just asking for things—although that certainly is part of it. Far more importantly, prayer is talking with God. It's getting close to and spending time with the one you love. It's seeking Him first, touching Him, getting to know Him better, being with Him, and waiting in His presence. It's acknowledging Him as the source of power upon whom you can depend. It's taking the time to say, *Speak to my heart, Lord, and tell me what I need to hear.* It is partnering with Him. It is aligning our spirit with His to see that His perfect will is done. It is establishing ourselves and our lives as being connected to God.

We can't receive God's best for our lives, and we can't push back the things that were never God's will for us, except through prayer. We can't leave our life to chance. We have to pray about everything all the time, not just when things go wrong. We have to pray over anything that concerns us, no matter how big—"With God nothing will be impossible" (Luke 1:37)—or how small—"The very hairs of your head are all numbered" (Matt. 10:30).

Without reducing prayer to a formula, in this book I have outlined seven basic types of prayers that can bring lasting peace and positive change to your life. But please don't be inhibited by these categories. They are just that, categories and suggestions. And don't be concerned about prayer talk or church talk. The Bible tells us the basic qualification for prayer: "He who comes to God must believe that He is, and that He is a rewarder of those who diligently seek Him" (Heb. 11:6).

The more you pray, the more you will find to pray about, and the more you'll be led to pray for others. Don't allow discouragement over unanswered prayer to cause you to doubt that God has heard you. If you have received Jesus and are praying in His name, then God hears you, and something is happening whether you see it manifested in your life now or not. In fact, every time you pray, you're advancing God's purposes for you. Without prayer, the full purpose God has for you can't happen.

— STORMIE OMARTIAN

SEVEN

Prayers

The Prayer of

Confession

I said,
"I will confess my transgressions to the LORD,"
 and You forgave the iniquity of my sin.

—PSALM 32:5

Prayer of Con
The Prayer
r of Release
ayer of Submission
The Pray
Prayer of
Prayer of Promise
The Prayer of C
The Pra
Prayer of Prai

THE Prayer

OF CONFESSION

THE WORD *SIN* is an old archery term, meaning to miss the bull's-eye. Anything other than dead center is sin. So sin in our lives doesn't just mean robbing a liquor store, murdering someone, or playing cards on Sunday. It's much more than that. In fact, anything off the center of God's best and perfect will for our lives is sin. That takes in a lot of territory!

When sin is not confessed, it becomes a subtle growth—wrapping its tentacles around every part of our beings until we are paralyzed. The agony of its

weight is accurately described in the Bible by
King David:

> When I kept silent, my bones grew old
> Through my groaning all the day long.
> For day and night Your hand was heavy upon me;
> My vitality was turned into the drought of summer.
> I acknowledged my sin to You,
> And my iniquity I have not hidden.
> I said, "I will confess my transgressions to the LORD,"
> And You forgave the iniquity of my sin.
>
> PSALM 32:3–5

When sin is left unconfessed, a wall goes up
between you and God. Even though the sin may have
stopped, if it hasn't been confessed before the Lord, it
will still weigh you down, dragging you back toward
the past you are trying to leave behind. I know because
I used to carry around a bag of failures on my back
that was so heavy I could barely move. I didn't realize
how spiritually stooped over I had become. When I
finally confessed my sins, I actually felt the weight
being lifted.

All of us with deep emotional wounds from the past already suffer from low self-esteem, fear, and guilt. We mentally beat up on ourselves, tend to think the worst about our situations, and feel responsible for everything that goes wrong. It's true we can have times of feeling guilty for things we have done, but we don't have to be tortured by living endlessly in guilt. God provided the key to release us from that: the prayer of confession.

Often we fail to see ourselves as responsible for certain actions. For example, while it's not your fault that someone abused you, your *reaction* to it now is your responsibility. You may feel justified in your anger or bitterness, but you must still confess it because it misses the mark of what God has for you. If you don't, its weight will eventually crush you.

THE PRAYER OF CONFESSION AND REPENTANCE

For confession to work, repentance must go along with it. *Repentance* literally means a change of mind. It means to turn your back, walk away, and decide not to do it again. It means getting your thinking aligned correctly with God. It's possible to confess without ever really conceding any fault at all. In fact, we can become simply good apologizers with no intent of being any other way. Confession and repentance mean saying, "This is my fault. I'm sorry about it, and I'm not going to do it anymore."

All sin has to be confessed and repented of for you to be free of bondage, whether you feel bad about it or not and whether you recognize it as sin or not. One day in my Christian counselor's office I confessed in prayer the two abortions I'd had even though I still had no concept at the time how wrong abortion was. I had always viewed abortion as a means of survival, not as a sin, but that did not make it right in God's eyes. I had read in the Bible about the value of life in the womb. I also read, "My conscience is clear, but that does not make me innocent" (1 Cor. 4:4 NIV). I was not free from the death grip of the guilt over those abortions until I repented and received God's full forgiveness.

Every time you confess something, check to see if you honestly and truly do not want to do that anymore. And remember, God "knows the secrets of the heart" (Ps. 44:21). Being repentant doesn't necessarily mean you will never do it again, but it does mean you don't *intend* to do it again. If you find that you are committing the same sin over and over, you need to confess it each time. If you have committed a sin that you just confessed the day before, don't let that come between you and God. Confess it again. As long as you are truly repentant each time, you will be forgiven and eventually set free. The Bible says, "Repent therefore and be converted, that your sins may be blotted out, so that times of refreshing may come from the presence of the Lord" (Acts 3:19).

> *Blessed is he whose transgression is forgiven.* PSALM 32:1

The devil has a hook in you wherever there is unconfessed sin. Repeated returns to the same sin are no excuse for not confessing. You must keep your life totally open before the Lord if you want to be delivered from the bondage of sin.

You can't be delivered from something you have not put out of your life. Confessing is speaking the whole truth about your sin. Renouncing is taking a firm stand against it and removing its right to stay. Because we are not perfect, confession and repentance are ongoing. There are always new levels of Jesus' life that need to be worked in us. We fall short of the glory of God in ways that we can't yet even imagine.

THE PRAYER OF CONFESSION HEALS YOUR HEART

When you are building a foundation, you have to dig out the dirt. The trouble is, most of us don't go deep enough. While you can't see all your errors all the time, you can have a heart that is willing to be taught by the Lord. Ask God to bring to light sins you are not aware of so they can be confessed, repented of, and forgiven. Recognize that there is something to confess every day and pray frequently as David did:

> See if there is any wicked way in me, and lead me in the way everlasting. (Ps. 139:24)
>
> Create in me a clean heart, O God, and renew a steadfast spirit within me. (Ps. 51:10)
>
> Cleanse me from secret faults. (Ps. 19:12)

Sometimes when we don't think we have anything to confess, praying for God's revelation will reveal an unrepentant attitude, such as criticism or unforgiveness, that has taken root in the heart. Confessing it keeps us from having to pay the emotional, spiritual, and physical price for it. It will also benefit our social lives since the imperfections in our personalities that we can't see are often obvious to others.

Confession is really a way of life. If we're not walking God's way, if we're doing anything in disobedience—gossiping, lying, or speaking in a degrading manner to someone—we need to clear the slate, and that only comes with confession: *God, I come before You and I confess my attitude toward my boss. I repent of that attitude. I want to become more like Christ every day.*

Sometimes when my husband, Michael, would say something that hurt my feelings, I would react—and say something equally as offensive back. This only made the strife worse. I soon learned that before I apologized to Michael, I had to apologize to God. I would go before the Lord and say, "God, I'm sorry for what I said. I know I was moving in the flesh and not the Spirit." I found that confessing to the Lord helped me to stop the behavior and be able to apologize to Michael with a better attitude.

Think about your own life. Has anything like that happened between you and another person? Do you have any attitude that you need to confess? If so, don't hesitate. The sooner you take care of it the better.

He who covers his sins will not prosper, but whoever confesses and forsakes them will have mercy. PROVERBS 28:13

Sin leads to death; repentance leads to life. How much time passes between the sin and the repentance will account for how much death is reaped in your life. If you've reaped a lot of death, the problems don't go away immediately when you confess. But your confession has started the process of reversing what has taken place as a result of the sin.

Always keep in mind that God's ways are for your benefit. Confession is not for Him to find out something. God already knows. Confession is for you to be made whole. God is not standing over you, waiting to punish you for what you do wrong. He doesn't have to because the punishment is inherent in the sin. Because God knows this, He has given you the key of confession. People who confess find mercy and God's unlimited power.

The Prayer of

Salvation

Our God is the God of salvation.

—Psalm 68:20

Prayer of Con

The Prayer

r of Release

ayer of Submission

The Pray

Prayer

Prayer of Promise

The Prayer of C

The Pra

Pray of

Prayer of Prai

THE Prayer

I'VE SPENT MANY YEARS learning to understand what was accomplished when Jesus died on the cross, and it simply means that *Jesus took all that I have coming to me—pain, sickness, failure, confusion, hatred, rejection, and death—and gave me all that He had coming to Him—all His wholeness, healing, love, acceptance, peace, joy, and life.* Because of God's grace, we can pray the prayer of salvation. All we have to do is say, "Jesus come live in me and be Lord over my life."

In my early twenties my lifestyle was motivated by a desperate need for love. One disastrous by-product of this lifestyle was two abortions in less than two years. Both were ugly, frightening, and physically and emotionally traumatic (not to mention illegal at the time), yet I felt relief more than remorse about them. Only years later after I began to walk with the Lord and learn of His ways, did I see what I had done.

When Michael and I decided to have a baby, month after month went by and I didn't get pregnant. I, who had gotten pregnant so easily before, thought surely I was being punished for the abortions.

"God, I know I don't deserve to give birth to new life after twice destroying life within me." I prayed. "But please have mercy and help me to conceive."

He answered that prayer, and my two children have been the greatest example of God's mercy and grace to me. *He gave me exactly what I did not deserve.*

THE PRAYER OF SALVATION BRINGS GOD'S MERCY AND GRACE

God's grace is for those who live in His kingdom and whose kingdom lives in them. We can't receive His grace unless we receive *Him*. It's a gift that is with Him, in His hand.

Grace and mercy are much alike. *Grace happens when God refrains from punishing a person who is guilty. Mercy is God's compassion for our misery beyond what may be expected.* We need both.

If it weren't for God's grace *and* mercy, we wouldn't even be saved for the Bible tells us, "by grace you have

> The LORD *takes pleasure in those who fear Him, in those who hope in His mercy.* PSALM 147:11

been saved" (Eph. 2:8) and "according to His mercy He saved us" (Titus 3:5). Before we met Jesus we were "guilty" and "miserable," but His "grace" and "mercy" have saved us.

Grace has to do with it all being *Him*. He does it. Not us. Grace is always a surprise. You think it's not going to happen, and it does.

The Prayer of Salvation Brings Entry into the Kingdom of God

Salvation is more than something Jesus did for us on the Cross of Calvary; it is Jesus living in us. You may have been born into a Christian family or have attended a Christian church all your life, but if you haven't prayed the prayer of salvation and told God that you want to receive Jesus as your Savior, you haven't been born into the kingdom of God. You can't inherit it; get it by osmosis, transplant, or implant; or wish upon a star for it. You have to declare *your* faith in Jesus Christ.

If you want Jesus' life in you, just say, "Jesus, I acknowledge You this day. I believe You are the Son of God as You say You are. Although it's hard to comprehend love so great, I believe You laid down your life for me so that I might have life eternally and abundantly now. I ask You to forgive me for not living Your way. I need You to help me become all You created me to be. Come into my life and fill me with Your Holy Spirit. Let all the death in me be crowded out by the power of Your presence and this day turn my life into a new beginning."

If you don't feel comfortable with this prayer, then talk to Jesus as you would to a good friend, and confess you've made some mistakes. Tell Him you can't live without Him. Ask Him to forgive you and come into your heart. Tell Him you receive Him as Lord, and thank Him for His eternal life and forgiveness.

Once you have prayed the prayer of salvation, you are released from guilt, your future is secure, and you are saved from death in every part of your life.

Jesus said to him, "I am the way, the truth, and the life. No one comes to the Father except through Me." JOHN 14:6

THE PRAYER OF SALVATION BRINGS FREEDOM FROM GUILT

Everyone has some kind of guilt for mistakes of the past. Sometimes it's for things we know we've done, sometimes it's deep regret over what we fear we could have prevented, and sometimes it's for violation of certain natural laws we're not even aware of violating. Whatever the reason, the load of guilt sits on us with crushing weight, and unless it's eliminated it separates us from the fullness of life.

What can ever take our guilt away? Consider, for instance, the man who accidentally backed a car over his two-year-old daughter and killed her. Or the woman who took drugs when she was pregnant and gave birth to a brain-damaged child. What about the mother who accidentally shot and killed her teenage son when he came home late one night and she thought he was a robber? How do these people find freedom from guilt over such devastating and irreparable damage?

Or how do you and I live with painful regrets? "If only I'd . . ." "If I just hadn't . . ." These thoughts echo the agony of situations that can never be changed. It's done! And there's no way to live with the truth of it unless you push it down deep and never allow yourself to feel it again. Don't talk about it. Don't bring it up. The trouble with that is you think you're getting away with it until it starts to surface on its own. Then it comes out in the form of disease. Or perhaps it affects your mind and emotions, making you angry or withdrawn or phobic or depressed like an infection of a deep wound that was quickly bandaged over without being cleaned and properly treated.

Or what about our guilt over things we've done that violated God's laws, laws of which we weren't aware at the time? No matter how much a woman who has had an abortion believes her decision was right, I've never heard one say, "I've been fulfilled and enriched by this experience." She may feel relieved of a burden, but she never thinks, "What a wonderful thing I've done. I know I have truly realized God's purpose for my life and I am a better person because of it." Acknowledged or not, the guilt is there because she has violated a law of nature.

What and who can take this guilt away? A friend's saying "Don't worry about it. . . . It wasn't your fault. . . . You can't blame yourself" never gets rid of what you feel inside. Only God's forgiveness can do that. When we pray the prayer of salvation to receive Jesus as our Savior, we are immediately released from the penalty of our past mistakes. For the first time we are free from having to face the failure of our past.

THE PRAYER OF SALVATION BRINGS PEACE AND ABUNDANT LIFE

When you pray to receive Jesus as your Savior, you have the peace of knowing that your future is secure. God's Word says, "Everyone who sees the Son and believes in Him may have everlasting life; and I will raise him up at the last day" (John 6:40). Your future in this life is also secure. God promises that if you acknowledge Him as Savior, He will guide you safely where you need to go: "In all your ways acknowledge Him, and He shall direct your paths" (Prov. 3:6). This doesn't mean that we will instantly have all our problems solved and never again know pain, but we will have the power within us to reach our full potential.

When Jesus died on the cross, He also rose from the dead to break the power of death over anyone who receives His life. Jesus conquered death—whether at the end of life or in the multiple ways that we face death daily. In the death of our dreams, finances, health, or relationships, Jesus can bring His life to resurrect any dead place in us. Therefore we don't have to feel hopeless. He also gives to everyone who opens up to Him a quality of life that is meaningful, abundant, and fulfilling. He transcends our every limitation and boundary and enables us to do things we never would have been capable of aside from Him. He is the only one who can give us life before death as well as life hereafter. Without Him we die a little every day. With Him as our Savior we become more and more alive.

The Prayer of Salvation Gives Entrance to the Holy Spirit

The Holy Spirit is the Spirit of God sent by Jesus to give us comfort, to build us up, to guide us in all truth, to bring us spiritual gifts, to help us pray more effectively, and to give us wisdom and revelation. The Holy Spirit is not a vapor or a mystical cloud; He is another part of God. He is God's power and the means by which God speaks to us.

The Bible says, "I will put My Spirit within you and cause you to walk in My statutes, and you will keep My judgments and do them" (Ezek. 36:27). The Holy Spirit works the wholeness of God into our lives. And there need be no fear or mystery about this because we alone of God's creation have a special place built in us where His Spirit can reside. That place will always be empty until it is filled with Him.

We don't want to have "a form of godliness" but deny "its power" (2 Tim. 3:5); denying God's power limits what God can do in our lives. Nor do we want to be "always learning and never able to come to the knowledge of the truth" (2 Tim. 3:7). Unless the Holy Spirit coaches us from within, our knowledge of the truth will always be limited. Don't limit what God can do in your life by failing to acknowledge His Holy Spirit in your life.

When I first heard the names Helper and Comforter in reference to the Holy Spirit, I knew immediately I wanted those attributes of God in my life. I realized that to get them, I first had to acknowledge the Holy Spirit's existence and then invite Him to reside within me. When I did that, I learned three important reasons to be filled with God's Holy Spirit:

to worship God more fully,
to experience and communicate God's love more completely,
to appropriate God's power in my life more effectively.

I have discovered over the years, however, that infilling of the Holy Spirit is ongoing and ever deepening. We have to be willing to open up to each new level and dimension so that He can enable us to accomplish what we could never do without this full measure of His love, power, and life.

The Prayer of

Release

*It is God who arms me with strength,
and makes my way perfect.*

—Psalm 18:32

Prayer of Conf

The Prayer

r of Release

ayer of Submission

The Pray

Prayer of

Prayer of Promise

The Prayer of C

The Pra

Prayer of Prai

THE Prayer

OF RELEASE

"YOU'RE WORTHLESS, and you'll never amount to anything," my mother said as she pushed me into the little closet underneath the stairway and slammed the door. "Now stay in there until I can stand to see your face!" The sound of her footsteps faded as she walked down the small hallway back to the kitchen.

I wasn't really sure what I had done to warrant being locked in the closet again, but I knew it must be bad. I knew *I* must be bad, and I believed that all the negative things she had ever said about me were surely accurate. After all, she was my mother.

The closet was a small, rectangular storage area underneath the stairs where the dirty laundry was kept in an old wicker basket. I sat on top of the pile of clothes and pulled my feet in tight to eliminate the possibility of being touched by the mice that periodically streaked across the floor. I felt lonely, unloved, and painfully afraid as I waited in that dark hole for the seemingly endless amount of time it took for her to remember I was there or for my father to return, at which time she would make sure I was let out. Either event would mean my release from the closet and from the devastating feeling of being buried alive and forgotten.

As you can probably tell from just this one incident, I was raised by a mentally ill mother, and, among other atrocities, I spent much of my early childhood locked in a closet. Although certain people were aware of her bizarre behavior from time to time, her mental illness wasn't clearly identified until I was in my late teens. During all my growing-up years, my mother's extremely erratic behavior left me with feelings of futility, hopelessness, helplessness, and deep emotional pain. So much so that by the time I was a young woman I was still locked in a closet—-only the boundaries were emotional rather than physical. I was walled in by a deep, ever-present pain in my soul, which expressed itself through certain acts of self-destruction and a paralyzing fear that controlled my every breath.

Many years later I sat in front of Mary Anne, a Christian counselor, who told me I needed to forgive my mother if I wanted to find complete wholeness and healing. *Forgive someone who treated me with hatred and abuse? Someone who has ruined my life by making me into an emotional cripple? How can I?* I thought to myself, overwhelmed at the prospect of so great a task. I had already confessed my sins, and now my counselor was asking me to forgive my mother—all in the same counseling session.

"You don't have to *feel* forgiveness in order to say you forgive someone," Mary Anne explained. "Forgiveness is something you do out of obedience to the Lord because He has forgiven *you*. You have to be willing to say, 'God, I confess hatred for my mother, and I ask your forgiveness. I forgive her for everything she did to me. I forgive her for not loving me, and I release her into your hands.'"

As difficult as it was, I did as Mary Anne said because I wanted to forgive my mother even though I felt nothing close to that at the time. "God, I forgive my mother," I said at the end of the prayer. I knew that for me even to be able to say those words, the power of God must be working in my life. And I felt His love at that moment more than I ever had before.

I soon learned, however, that unforgiveness as deeply rooted as mine toward my mother must be unraveled, one layer at a time. This was especially true for me since my mother's verbal abused continued to increase in intensity as time went on. One day as I was again asking God to give me a forgiving heart, I felt led to pray, "Lord, help me to have a heart like *Yours* for my mother."

Almost immediately I had a vision of her I had never seen before. She was beautiful, fun loving, gifted, a woman who bore no resemblance to the person I knew. My understanding told me I was seeing her the way God had made her to be and not the way she had become. What an amazing revelation! I couldn't have conjured it up myself. Nothing surpassed my hatred for my mother, except perhaps the depth of my own emptiness. Yet now I felt compassion and sympathy for her.

In an instant I put together the pieces of her past—the tragic and sudden death of her mother when she was eleven, the suicide of her beloved uncle and foster father a few years later, her feelings of abandonment, guilt, bitterness, and unforgiveness which contributed to her emotional and mental illness. I could see how her life, like mine, had been twisted and deformed by circumstances beyond her control. Suddenly I no longer hated her for it. I felt sorry for her instead.

Being in touch with the heart of God for my mother brought such forgiveness in me that when she died a few years later, I had absolutely no bad feelings toward her. In fact, the more I forgave her, the more the Lord brought to mind good memories. I was amazed that there were any at all!

Forgiveness leads to life. Unforgiveness is a slow death. Forgiveness is ongoing because once you've dealt with the past, constant infractions occur in the present. None of us gets by without having our pride wounded or being manipulated, offended, or hurt by someone. Each time that happens it leaves a scar on the soul if not confessed, released, and dealt with before the Lord. Besides that, unforgiveness also separates you from people you love. They sense a spirit of unforgiveness, even if they can't identify it, and it makes them uncomfortable and distant.

You may be thinking, "I don't have to worry about this because I have no unforgiveness toward anyone." But forgiveness also has to do with not being critical of others. It has to do with keeping in mind that people are often the way they are because of how life has shaped them. It has to do with remembering that God is the only one who knows the whole story and therefore we never have the right to judge. Being chained in unforgiveness keeps you from the healing, joy, and restoration that are there for you. Being released into everything God has for you today and tomorrow means letting go of all that's happened in the past. It means praying a prayer of release.

THE PRAYER OF RELEASE BRINGS FREEDOM FROM BLAMING GOD

My husband and I have a friend who is gifted in many ways but he has shut God out of His life, blaming

Him for a car accident in which his sister was killed
and he was injured severely enough to end his
promising sports career. Years after that accident, he
still bitterly questions why God didn't keep it from
happening. The truth is, the accident was never part of
God's plan. It was the devil who came to destroy
because death *is* a part of *his* plan. Our friend is a good
man, but he is agonizingly frustrated and unfulfilled
because he has shut God off from working powerfully
in his life.

Blaming God is far more common than most of us
care to admit, especially for those who have been abused,
neglected, or deeply disappointed by authority figures.
The tendency is to think subconsciously of God as
being like that abusive father, grandparent, teacher, or
boss, projecting on Him attitudes and behavior that
have nothing to do with who He really is.

We also blame God for anything negative our
parents told us about ourselves. We feel God must have
created us the way they say we are and we wonder why
He was so careless. We also project human imperfections
onto Him. For example, we blame Him if our parents
didn't want or love us.

The lie we believe when we blame God is "God could have kept this from happening. He could have made things different." The truth is God has given us a free will, which He won't violate. As a result, we all make choices, and things are often the way they are because of those choices. God also gives us limitations and boundaries for our protection. If we will to violate that order, leaving our circumstance to chance or the work of the enemy, we breed destruction.

Blaming God is a no-win attitude. We back ourselves into a corner with no way out, instead of recognizing God as the only way out. Blaming God produces misplaced anger that will be channeled inward—making you sick, frustrated, and unfulfilled— or outward, causing you to hate a husband or wife, to abuse a child, to treat a friend rudely, to be uncooperative with a fellow worker, or to lash out at strangers.

To stop blaming God, we have to know what He is really like. And we can find out by looking to Jesus, who said, "He who has seen Me has seen the Father" (John 14:9). Unless we truly let Jesus penetrate every part of our lives, we won't ever really know what God is like.

When you truly know Jesus, you see that Father God is faithful and compassionate. His love is unlimited and unfailing. He does not neglect, abuse, forget, or misunderstand. He will never disappoint or be imperfect. When we understand who God really is and stop blaming Him, we find peace and security.

If you are mad at God, then you need to get to know Him better because there is a lot about Him that you don't fully understand. The best thing to do is to be honest with Him about it. You won't hurt God's feelings—He has known about it all along anyway. Pray to Him saying, "Father I have been angry at You because of this particular situation (be specific). I have hated this, and I've blamed you for it. Please forgive me and help me to be released from it. Take away my misconceptions about You and help me to know You better."

The opposite of blaming God is trusting Him. Decide now whom you will trust. You can't move into all God has for you if any bitterness and misplaced blame have a place in your heart. If you've been mad at God, say so. "God, I've been mad at You ever since my brother was killed in that accident." "God, I've been mad at You since my baby died." "God, I've been mad at You ever since I didn't get that job I prayed for." Be honest. You won't crush God's ego. Release the hurt and let yourself cry. Tears are freeing and healing. Pray a prayer of release, "Lord, I confess my hurt and my anger, and my hardness of heart toward You. I no longer hold that offense against You."

HERE ARE SEVEN VERSES TO REMIND YOU OF THE GOODNESS OF GOD. You can pray them as a prayer of release:

> Blessed are all those who put their trust in Him.
>
> PSALM 2:12
>
> He will deliver the needy when he cries.
>
> PSALM 72:12
>
> Those who seek the LORD shall not lack any
>   good thing.
>
> PSALM 34:10
>
> You are my help and my deliverer.
>
> PSALM 70:5
>
> I will make darkness light before them,
>   and crooked places straight.
>
> ISAIAH 42:16
>
> Surely God will never do wickedly, nor will the
>   Almighty pervert justice.
>
> JOB 34:12

The Lord will deliver me from every evil work and preserve me for His heavenly kingdom.

2 TIMOTHY 4:18

THE PRAYER OF RELEASE HELPS YOU TO FORGIVE OTHERS

Abuse is any unpleasant treatment that lowers self-worth—verbal abuse, neglect, a perceived lack of love—as well as beatings and molestation. If a child can't perceive his parents' acceptance of him, he grows up with a self-destructive hunger for love that can't be satisfied by any human being. The needs not met in childhood will be just as strong in adulthood, but they will be expertly camouflaged.

If you were abused as a child, don't be misled into saying to yourself, "I'm born-again—I shouldn't still hurt inside. There must be something wrong with me." The fact that you still hurt doesn't negate your born-again status or make you any less spiritual. Because people tend to view God the same way they viewed their parents, it takes a time of healing, deliverance, and getting to know the love of God before total trust comes.

Forgiving your parents is a big part of the healing (and crucial to avoiding the pitfall of abusing your own children). You have to forgive the father who never protected you, the mother who mistreated and abused you, the stepfather who didn't love you, the grandfather or uncle who sexually molested you, the parent who was never there or deserted you through death or abandonment, the weak parent who shut you out emotionally, the selfish parent who reminded you that you were never wanted, or the emotionally deficient parent who didn't know how to properly nurture you.

These bitterly painful experiences will *continue* to hurt you if you don't cry out your pain to the Lord, release all that pain and bitterness to Him, and ask Him to help you forgive. You will not only be hurt by your unforgiveness but, worse yet, you may well hurt your own children. For their sake, if not your own, you have to fully release the past.

Seeing your parent as the unloved, mistreated, or traumatized child he or she may have been can help you to forgive, yet most people know little about their parents' backgrounds. Most incidents, especially the bad ones, are seldom talked about, even by another relative.

When you understand that your parent did not deliberately withhold love from you, but actually never had it to give in the first place, it's easier to forgive. Sometimes what one parent *didn't* do hurts as bad as what the abusing one *did*. A parent's noninvolvement or unwillingness to step in and rescue you feels like a betrayal. Unforgiveness for that uninvolved parent is more difficult to recognize but is more common than we think. Ask God to show you any unforgiveness toward a parent who didn't come to your rescue. If it's there, you have to deal honestly with your feelings about it.

We all need parents who will love us, encourage us, nurture us, be affectionate with us, believe for the best in us, and be interested in what we do. Those of us who did not have parents like that have needs that only God can meet. We can't go back in time and get someone to hold and nurture us, and we mustn't demand it from a spouse or friends because they can't do it. It has to come from our heavenly Father.

God is our only hope for restoring damaged relationships. Praying a prayer of release for the hurt that has happened and praising God for His transformation of the situation is one of the avenues by which restoration will happen. In times of weakness when life seems out of control, choose to put yourself under God's control. Surrender your weak places fully and honestly to Him so He can turn them around to be vessels of His strength. He is a God of restoration and redemption, so He can redeem whatever has occurred in your past. He can mend the breach between you and your children, or parents, or friends. Restoration doesn't happen overnight, but redemption can. Allow God to redeem your situation now, so it can be turned around and headed in the right direction.

The Prayer of Release Is a Stairway to Wholeness

If you can't forgive another person it doesn't mean you aren't saved, and it doesn't mean you won't go to heaven. But it does mean you can't have all that God has for you and you will not be free of emotional pain.

The first step to forgiving is to *receive God's forgiveness* and let its reality penetrate the deepest part of our being. When we realize how much we have been forgiven, it's easier to understand that we have no right to pass judgment on one another. Being forgiven and released from everything we've ever done is such a miraculous gift, how could we refuse to obey God when He asks us to forgive others as He has forgiven us? Easy! We focus our thoughts on the person who has wronged us rather than on the God who makes all things right.

Forgiveness doesn't make the other person right, it makes you free.

Forgiveness is a two-way street. God forgives you, and you forgive others. God forgives you quickly and completely upon your confession of wrongdoing. You are to forgive others quickly and completely, whether they admit failure or not. Most of the time people don't feel they've done anything wrong anyway, and if they do, they certainly don't want to admit it to you. That is why we must release that person and the situation and the hurt to God in prayer.

Forgiveness is a choice that we make. We base our decision not on what we *feel* like doing but on what we *know* is *right*. I did not feel like forgiving my mother. Instead, I chose to forgive her because God's Word says, "Forgive, and you will be forgiven" (Luke 6:37). That verse also says that we shouldn't judge if we don't want to be judged ourselves. Instead, we are to release people and circumstances to God and let Him be the judge.

There are both spiritual and psychological reasons to forgive. The spiritual reason is that we desire to obey God, and He has told us to forgive others just as He has forgiven us: "Be kind to one another, tenderhearted, forgiving one another, just as God in Christ also forgave you" (Eph. 4:32). When we forgive people who have hurt us, we restore their God-given worth and value— not because they deserve it but because God has already done the same for us.

The psychological reason to forgive others is to free ourselves from the pain and the victimization that other people have inflicted on us. When we forgive, we make a choice to no longer allow other people's sin to dictate how we feel or what we do. Forgiveness gives us the freedom to truly live our lives as God intended.

It was hard for me to understand that God loves my mother as much as He loves me. He loves all people as much as He loves me. The most important thing to remember when it comes to forgiving is that forgiveness doesn't make the other person right, it makes you free. The best way to turn anger, bitterness, hatred, and resentment for someone into love is to pray for that person. God softens your heart when you do and brings wholeness into your life.

The Prayer of

Submission

Show me Your ways, O LORD;
teach me Your paths.

—PSALM 25:4

The Prayer of Submission

The Prayer

Prayer of Promise

The Prayer of C

The Pr

Prayer of Prai

THE *Prayer*

WHEN I FIRST RECEIVED JESUS into my heart,
I showed Him into the guest room. The problem was,
He wasn't content to stay there. He kept knocking on
one door after another until I was opening doors to
rooms I had never even known were there. He exposed
every dark corner of each room to His cleansing light.
I soon realized that He wanted me to acknowledge Him
as Lord over *every* area of my life.

One such room in my heart was the issue of having children. I married my husband, Michael, about three years after I received Jesus, and because so much was happening in our lives at that time, we never really discussed children. I had a million reasons for not wanting any, not the least of which was the fear that I would perpetuate my own crippled upbringing. I couldn't bear to watch myself destroy an innocent life. As God knocked on one door after another—finances, marriage, attitudes, appearance, friendships—I opened up to His lordship. Yet I turned a deaf ear as He tapped relentlessly at the door of motherhood, which was dead-bolted by my selfishness and fear. The knocking persisted, however, challenging my daily "Jesus, be Lord over every area of my life" prayer.

One morning about a year after we were married, friends stopped us before church to show off their new son. As I held him briefly, I had a vision of holding a child of my own. Later in church I thought about that moment, and the possibility of having a baby suddenly seemed pleasant.

Okay, Lord, I thought, *if we're really supposed to have a child, let me hear something to that effect from Michael.* With that I put the matter totally out of my mind.

Later that afternoon, Michael turned to me and said, "That baby you were holding this morning before church was so cute. Maybe we should have one of our own."

"What?" I said in disbelief. "Are you serious?"

"Sure. Why not? Isn't that what people do?" he asked.

"Yes, but I've never heard you say anything like that before."

Remembering my quick prayer that morning, I prayed silently, *Lord, it's frightening how fast You can work sometimes. May Your perfect will be done in my life.*

Even though I was still fearful and apprehensive, I knew the time had come when God was going to bring life to a place in me that had died years before. I sensed that allowing Him to be Lord over this area would be a major part of the redemption of all that had been lost in my life.

When you invite Jesus into the home of your being (being born again), you are supposed to also give Him the run of the house (making Him Lord over your life). However, many of us are slow to do that completely. Whether we admit it or not, we hesitate to believe that God can be trusted with every area of our lives.

The Bible says,

Trust in the LORD with *all* your heart,
And lean not on your own understanding;
In *all* your ways acknowledge Him,
And He shall direct your paths.

(PROVERBS 3:5–6, EMPHASIS ADDED)

Notice that word *all*. It's very specific. If we want things to work out well, we have to acknowledge Him as Lord over all areas of our lives. I had to be willing to give God the right-of-way by frequently saying, "Jesus, be Lord over every area of my life." Then as He pointed to places where I had not opened the door to His rulership, I let Him in.

I know now that God does this with all people who invite Him to dwell in their lives.

THE PRAYER OF SUBMISSION BRINGS GOD'S BENEFITS

Some people give God total access to the home of their being right away. Others leave Him standing in the entryway indefinitely. Many people do as I did and allow Him to gain entrance slowly. When He knocks on different doors inside you, just know that He will never bulldoze His way in and break down the walls. He will simply knock persistently and quietly, and as He's invited, will come to gently occupy each corner of your life to clean and rebuild.

He has given you a choice. Will you choose to open up and share every part of yourself with Him and let Him reign in your life? This is the prayer of submission to His will.

God doesn't enforce obedience or submission. We often wish He would because it would be easier, but He gives us the choice. I have had to ask Him to teach me to be obedient out of love for Him and the desire to serve the One who has done so much for me. If you want the same benefits, you have to do the same thing.

It helps to understand that the Lord is on your side and the call to obedient submission is not to make you feel like a hopeless failure if you don't do everything right. Knowing that God asks you to live a certain way for your own benefit because He knows life only works out right for you when it is lived on His terms will help you desire to know His ways and to live in them. You start the process by being willing to say "God, I don't want anything to separate me from Your presence and love. And I really do have a heart that wants to submit and obey. Please show me where I am not living in obedience, and help me to do what I need to do to be submissive to You."

The minute we take one step of obedience, God opens up opportunities for new life.

THE PRAYER OF SUBMISSION BRINGS REST

Rest is an "anchor of the soul" (Heb. 6:19), which keeps us from being tossed around on the sea of circumstance. It's not just the feeling of ease we get from a vacation or the relaxation of a sound sleep at night; true rest is a place inside ourselves where we can be still and know that He is God, no matter what appears to be happening around us.

Jesus says, "Come to Me, all you who labor and are heavy laden, and I will give you rest" (Matt. 11:28).

He instructs us not to allow our hearts to be troubled but to resist this by deciding to rest in quiet submission to Him and His will. We must say, "God, I choose this day to enter into the rest you have for me. Show me how."

When we do that, God reveals all that stands in our way. Resting is "casting all your care upon Him, for He cares for you" (1 Pet. 5:7) and learning to be content no matter what the circumstances (Phil. 4:11)—not necessarily being delighted with the circumstances but being able to say, "God is in charge, I have prayed about it, He knows my need, I am obeying in submission to the best of my knowledge. I can rest."

When our hearts turn from what we know of living the way God intended us to live, we lose our place of rest. When we pray and live out the prayer of submission and quiet trust, we find the gift of God's rest.

The Prayer of Submission Releases Your Dreams

I always wanted to be a successful entertainer. It sounds embarrassingly shallow even to mention it now, but it was a desperate drive at the time. I desired to be famous and respected, never mind the fact that I possibly didn't have what it might take to attain either. After I received the Lord and had been married just a few months, God clearly impressed upon my heart that I wasn't to be doing television or commercials anymore. I wasn't sure why, but I knew it wasn't right for me. Whenever my agent presented me with an interview I once would have died for, the thought of it gave me a hollow, uneasy,

> We must be willing to give God the complete right-of-way in our lives.

deathlike feeling. Because the peace of God did not accompany the prospect of doing it, I turned down every job I was offered.

Yes, God, I won't do that commercial. Yes, God, I won't accept another television show. Yes, God, I won't sing in clubs anymore. Yes, God, I'll leave the agency.

Gradually, all my work was gone. God had closed all doors and asked me to stop knocking on the ones that were not in His plan for me. The experience was scary, but looking back now I clearly see the reasons for it. Acting was an idol for me. I did it entirely for the attention and acceptance it would bring me, not because I loved the work. My identity was totally wrapped up in what I did. For God to change that, He had to take away my means of defining who I thought I was and help me to establish my identity in Jesus. He knew I couldn't be healed of my deep inferiority feelings if I was daily putting myself in a position of being judged by superficial standards.

The part we don't want to hear is that a time comes when each of us must place our desires and dreams in the hands of God that He might free us from those that are not in His will. In other words, you secure your future by allowing your dream to die and God's plan to replace it. If you've always had a certain picture of what you think you should do, you have to be willing to let the picture be destroyed. It is an act of submitting your desires to the will of God. If it really is what God has for you, He will raise you up to do that and more. If it isn't, you will be frustrated as long as you cling to it. Often the desires of your heart are the desires of His heart, but they still must be achieved through submission to His way, not yours, and you must know He is accomplishing them in you, not you achieving them yourself.

God wants us to stop holding onto our dreams and start holding onto Him so that He can enable us to soar above ourselves and our own limitations. Whenever we let go of what we long for, God will bring it back to us in another dimension.

Whoever desires to save his life will lose it, but whoever loses his life for My sake will save it. LUKE 9:24

THE PRAYER OF SUBMISSION BRINGS FULFILLMENT

How many times do we ask God to give us what we want, but we don't want to give God what He wants? We lack what we desire most—wholeness, peace, fulfillment, and joy—because we are not obedient and submissive to God.

Often we are not obedient because we don't understand that God has set up certain rules to protect us and to work for our benefit. He designed us and knows what will fulfill us most. Even the Ten Commandments were not given to instill guilt, but as an umbrella of blessing and protection from the rain of evil. If we choose to live outside the arena of blessing, we suffer the consequences. Spiritual darkness and confusion then have access to our lives, and we are drained of God's best.

When we obey in submission to God's will, life has simplicity and clarity and unlimited blessing. We need God's laws because we don't know how to make life work without them.

The law was given in the Old Testament to show us that we can't possibly fulfill it in terms of *human* energy, but must depend on God. We need His power to escape the death syndrome that surrounds us. The Bible says that Noah was given new life because he did all that God asked him to do (Gen. 6:22). That word *all* seems frightening when it comes to obedience because we know ourselves well enough to doubt we can do it all. And the truth is we can't. But we can take steps in the right direction and watch God do it as we yield ourselves in submission to Him.

THE PRAYER OF SUBMISSION BRINGS GREAT REWARD

"When will I ever get to the point where I no longer hurt inside?" I asked God one day in prayer. Even though I had been set free from depression and my life was far more stable than it had ever been, I still lived on an emotional roller coaster. My questions to God during that time went on and on:

"When will I stop feeling like a failure?"

"When will I not be devastated by what other people say to me?"

"When will I not view every hint of misfortune as the end of the world?"

As I read the Bible one morning, my eyes fell on the words, "Why do you call Me 'Lord, Lord' and not do the things which I say?" (Luke 6:46). The passage went on to explain that anyone who hears the words of the Lord and does *not* put them into practice is building a house with no foundation. When the storm comes, it will collapse and be completely destroyed.

Could it be that I'm getting blown over and destroyed by every wind of circumstance that comes my way because I'm not doing what the Lord says to do in some area? I wondered. I knew I was building on solid rock (Jesus), and I had been laying a strong foundation (in the Word, prayer, praise, confession, and ongoing forgiveness) but it appeared that this

When we obey God's will, life has simplicity and clarity.

foundation could only be stabilized and protected through my obedience.

I searched the Bible for more information, and every place I turned I read more about the reward of obeying God:

"Blessed are those who hear the word of God and keep it!" (Luke 11:28)

"No good thing will He withhold from those who walk uprightly." (Ps. 84:11)

"Behold, I set before you today a blessing and a curse; the blessing, if you obey the commandments of the Lord your God which I command you today." (Deut. 11:26–27)

> *Even if God doesn't love the way we live, He still loves us.*

The more I read, the more I saw the link between *obedience* and the *presence of God*. "If anyone loves Me, he will keep My word; and My Father will love him, and We will come to him and make our home with him" (John 14:23). I was already convinced by this time that I could only find wholeness and restoration in His presence, so this promise that my obedience would open the door to God's dwelling with me was particularly impressive.

I also saw a definite connection between *obedience* and the *love of God*. "If anyone obeys his Word, God's love is truly made complete in him (1 John 2:5 NIV). According to the Bible, God doesn't stop loving us if we don't obey. Even if He doesn't love the way we live, He still loves us. But we are unable to feel or enjoy that love fully if we're not living as God intended us to live, in total submission to His Word and His will.

The Prayer of

Praise

From the rising of the sun to its going down
the LORD's name is to be praised.

—PSALM 113:3

Prayer of Con
The Prayer
er of Release
ayer of Submission
The Pray
Prayer of Promise
The Prayer of C
The Pra
Prayer of Pra

THE
Prayer

I USED TO HURRY INTO THE CHURCH twenty minutes late on Sunday morning. By the time I found a seat and settled into it, the worship and praise time was over and the pastor was preaching. I wasn't concerned about this because I was there for the teaching. Yet my mind wandered everywhere and didn't settle into the message until the sermon was half over.

On the days I arrived in plenty of time to get a seat before the service started and was a full participant through the entire worship time, I found I was open to receive the message as if God were speaking directly to me. My heart was made soft and receptive to what the Holy Spirit wanted to teach me because of the twenty or thirty minutes I had spent praising God. Negative attitudes I had come in with were melted away and replaced with ones more in alignment with what God desired. I was made ready and open to receive from God.

Worship invites God's presence, and that's where deliverance happens. Two men in prison were singing praises to God when suddenly the prison doors flew open and their chains fell off (Acts 16:26). In the spirit realm when we praise the Lord, the prison doors of our lives are opened, our bonds are broken, and we are set free. Praising God opens you to experience His love, and it will liberate you.

The Prayer of Praise Brings Healing and Transformation

The more time we spend praising the Lord, the more we will see ourselves and our circumstances grow in wholeness. That's because praise softens our hearts and makes them pliable. It also covers us protectively. The more the pliability and covering are maintained, the more quickly our hearts can be molded and healed.

Praise and worship of God are always acts of will. We have to *will* to praise God even when we don't feel like it. Sometimes our problems or the burdens we carry choke out our good intentions, so we have to make the effort to establish praise as a way of life. And it becomes a way of life when we make it our *first* reaction to what we face and not a last resort. *Now* is the time to lift up a prayer of praise to God for everything in your life. Thank Him for His Word, His faithfulness, His love, His grace, His healing. Thank Him for what He has done for you personally. Keep in mind that whatever you thank the Lord for—peace, financial blessing, health, a new job, an end to depression—will start the process of its being released to you at that time.

In the Old Testament, the people who carried the Ark of the Covenant stopped every six steps to worship. We also have to remind ourselves not to go very far without stopping to praise and worship. For emotional healing and restoration, we have to be six-step persons and continually invite the presence of the Lord to rule in our situations.

THE PRAYER OF PRAISE ALIGNS US WITH GOD'S PURPOSES

Without praise we experience an eroding that leads to bondage and death. The Bible says, "Although they knew God, they did not glorify Him as God, nor were thankful, but became futile in their thoughts, and their foolish hearts were darkened" (Rom. 1:21). *With* praise, you and your circumstances can be changed, because it gives God entrance into every area of your life and allows Him to be enthroned there.

So any time you struggle with negative emotions, such as anger, unforgiveness, fear, hurt, oppression, depression, self-hatred, or worthlessness, thank God that He is bigger than all that. Thank Him that His plans and purposes for you are good. Thank Him that in any weak area of your life, He will be strong. Thank Him that He came to restore you. Remember the names of the Lord, and use them in your prayer. "I praise You, Lord, because You are my Deliverer and Redeemer." "Thank You, God, that You are my Healer and Provider."

Once you align yourself with God's purposes through praise, you can claim things that you can't see yet in your life as though they were there. "Lord, I have absolutely no way to make my healing come about, but You are all powerful and can make it happen. I thank You and praise You for Your healing power in my life." Doing this is your greatest weapon against the feelings of inadequacy, purposelessness, and futility that can undermine all God has made you to be.

Remember. Praise lifts us powerfully into God's presence and aligns us with His purposes.

THE PRAYER OF PRAISE DEFEATS CRITICISM

There is another reason why the prayer of praise and thanksgiving is so vital to our walk with God. It crowds out criticism, which I discovered many years ago not only limits what God can do in my life but invites judgment back upon myself.

Let me explain. Those of us who have been abused as children often grow up to be judgmental and critical. Being torn down when we were young makes tearing someone else down to build ourselves up very appealing. We become unmerciful because we were not shown mercy.

Criticizing others quickly becomes a bad habit that can backfire. Constantly criticizing, even only in the mind, invites a critical spirit. When you have a spirit of criticism, your every thought and word is colored by it. You eventually become cynical and then completely unable to experience joy. You can be reading the Word, praying, and obeying and still not have peace and joy in your life because you are critical. Being critical of circumstances or conditions can be as detrimental as criticizing people because it turns you into a grumbler

Mercy triumphs over judgment.

JAMES 2:13

and complainer—the type of person people generally like to avoid. It's difficult to find the love and support you need when no one wants to be around you.

Criticism crowds love out of our hearts. "Though I have the gift of prophecy, and understand all mysteries and all knowledge, and though I have all faith, so that I could remove mountains, but have not love, I am nothing" (1 Cor. 13:2). Without love in our hearts we cannot grow emotionally, and we will always be at a standstill in our healing and development. But we can overcome a critical attitude by being constantly filled with the love of the Lord through prayerful praise and thanksgiving toward Him.

THE PRAYER OF PRAISE DEFEATS DEPRESSION

The prayer of praise and thanksgiving can also lift you out of hopeless feelings of depression. Being depressed is a sign that your personality has turned inward and focused on itself. One of the healthiest steps to take is to focus outwardly on God through praise. Stop everything you're doing and say, "Lord, I praise You. I worship You. I give thanks to You. I glorify You. I love You." Thanking Him for everything you can think of is the best way to stop the stream of self-abuse that goes through your head.

It says in God's Word that "anxiety in the heart of man causes depression, but a good word makes it glad" (Prov. 12:25). The good word that will truly make your heart glad comes from the Lord through His Word. When you pray the prayer of praise and thanksgiving, pray God's Word. Find verses of Scripture that speak praise and say them out loud. When you find a promise or word from God that speaks to your situation, continually speak it aloud with thanksgiving; eventually your spirit and soul will respond to the hope and truth of God's Word.

THE PRAYER OF PRAISE DEFEATS FEAR

Before I received Jesus, fear was the controlling factor of my life: fear of failure, of bodily harm, of being emotionally hurt, of getting old, of being a nobody. An aching, paralyzing, all-engulfing spirit of fear had overtaken me, bringing with it companion spirits of suicide, despair, anxiety, and hopelessness. As I fought to keep from drowning in my fears, I ran out of strength. Gradually my fear of life overrode my fear of death, and suicide seemed as if it would be a pleasant relief.

I have heard it said many times that F-E-A-R stands for:

> **F**alse
>
> **E**vidence
>
> **A**ppearing
>
> **R**eal

The devil presents false evidence and makes it seem real. We can choose to listen to his falsehoods or believe

God. The prayer of praise is your greatest weapon against fear, so use it with great force. Clap your hands, sing, and speak praises to God. Thank Him for His great love. The more you do, the more you'll open up to receive it. God's love and fear cannot reside in the same heart!

No matter what has happened to you in the past or what's happening in the world around you, God promises to protect you as you walk with Him now. In fact, He is

There is no fear in love; but perfect love casts out fear, because fear involves torment. 1 JOHN 4:18

committed to protecting you all the time. We don't understand how much evil the Lord protects us from every day, but I'm sure it's far more than we imagine. He is more powerful than any adversary we face, and He promises that no matter what the enemy brings into our lives, we will triumph in it.

The only fear you are to have is the fear of God, a respect for God's authority and power. Fearing God means fearing what life without Him would be and thanking Him continually that because of His love you'll never have to experience it.

THE PRAYER OF PRAISE DEFEATS SELFISHNESS

The opposite of focusing inward on self is focusing outward on God. How opposite this is from what the world promotes today! We mistakenly think that an intense focus on ourselves will contribute most to our happiness and fulfillment, when actually the opposite is true. Dwelling on ourselves leads to emotional sickness. Instead of being filled with thoughts about what we need and feel, we must be full of the Lord and thankful to Him that He meets all our needs better than we can.

The only focus inward we are to have is sincere self-examination, to see if we are living and thinking God's way. Even then, that should be done in God's presence because He is the only one who can reveal the truth in a way that convicts but does not condemn.

Our complete focus must be on God alone. And the best way to focus on God is to thank Him continually for all He has given, praise Him for all He has done, and worship Him for all He is. It's impossible to be self-absorbed or self-obsessed while you are glorifying and praising God!

THE PRAYER OF PRAISE BUILDS PATIENCE

There will be times when your prayers will not be answered—at least not exactly according to your timetable. Part of standing strong in times of unanswered prayer is waiting, and waiting produces patience. When you are patient, you are able to take control of your very being and place yourself in God's hands. He, then, is in control whether it is night or day in your soul. He becomes God to you in every season of your life—the good and the bad. And because you know Him that way, you become unshakable.

Since we have no choice but to wait, our attitude makes a lot of difference. The best way to sustain a good attitude while you wait is to spend much time in praise and worship of God. Say, "Lord, I praise You in the midst of this situation. I confess I'm afraid that my prayers may never be answered. I'm weary and discouraged from the waiting, and feel I'm losing the strength to fight.

Forgive me, Lord, for not trusting You more. Help me to hear Your voice and follow Your lead. Thank You that You are in full control."

The prayer of praise is a way of reminding ourselves that God hears our every prayer. Even when we feel like nothing is going on, in God's kingdom God's love, healing, and redemption are always going on.

THE PRAYER OF PRAISE BUILDS SELF-ESTEEM

God created each one of us to be somebody and no life is an accident or unwanted in His eyes. He has given us each a distinct purpose or calling. High self-esteem means seeing yourself as God made you, recognizing that you are a unique person in whom He has placed specific gifts, talents, and purpose unlike anyone else. When you allow God to show you what He thinks of you and let it sink in and penetrate every fiber of your being, whatever is added or taken away doesn't make or break you.

I have learned to value myself as God values me by deliberately thanking and praising Him for any positive things I see. "Thank you, Lord, that I am alive, that I can walk, that I can talk, that I can see, that I can prepare a meal, that I can write letters, that I am neat, that I love my children, that I know Jesus." As we praise God for specific things, we are inviting His presence to bring transformation. It's the best medicine I know for believing lies about yourself.

For example, like most people who have been scarred by verbal abuse in early childhood, I have been highly oversensitive to other people's comments. This is a negative trait. Someone who is easily hurt puts others in the uncomfortable position of having to walk on eggshells or be responsible for hurting them. By praising God in the midst of my oversensitivity, I have allowed Him to transform that negative quality into a positive one—that of being sensitive to other people instead of myself.

When the devil tries to deceive you with lies about yourself, when he tries to tear you down, ignore his taunts and praise God for who you are in Him!

The Prayer of

Promise

There has not failed one word
of all His good promise.

—1 Kings 8:56

Prayer of Con

The Prayer

Prayer of Release

ayer of Submission

The Pra

Prayer

The Pray

Prayer of

Prayer of Promise

The Prayer of C

The Pr

Prayer of Prai

THE Prayer

I HAD BEEN A SINGER and an actress on television for about three years when I was asked to sing on a series of recording sessions for a Christian musical. I wasn't a Christian so I had no idea what one was. My friend Terry was the contractor on this session, which meant she was in charge of hiring all the singers. She was one of the best studio singers in Los Angeles, and I had worked with her often. She always sang the lead, and I would stand next to her and sing second.

On our lunch break we went out together in a large group, and I learned that everyone on the session was a Christian except me. They all talked about their futures, some of which seemed to be even more precarious than mine. Yet none of them feared the future as I did. They said that God had a plan for their lives and as long as they walked in the will of God, their futures were secure in His hands. I had never heard of such a thing.

Each day of the sessions I found myself increasingly attracted to the sense of purpose these people had. *I wonder if God has a plan for my life?* I thought to myself. That would mean I didn't have to make life happen. I thought about this for the next few days of the sessions. And I tried to learn more from each of the singers at every lunch break without letting them know why I was interested. I didn't want anyone pressuring me to have a life of purpose.

As I was on my way home from the last session on the final day, I prayed to this God of theirs without knowing if He could even hear me. "God, if You have a plan for my life," I said, "I need to know what it is and what to do about it."

I heard no reply. As I suspected, this God would probably never listen to someone like me. Yet over the course of the next few months many things happened to me, one of which changed my life forever: I met the God that Terry and her friends had been talking about. The simple prayer I had prayed in the car, to a God I didn't even know, was answered.

Many years have gone by from that day I decided to receive the Lord. In that time, God has kept His promises, and He has always come through. Many times it didn't feel as if He was going to, but He did. It certainly hasn't been the way I was trying to direct Him each time or as quickly as I wanted to see things happen. And, thank God, it wasn't to the degree I envisioned. It was always far better. His timing was perfect and His way was right! Everything I have received from the Lord and more, I want for you. That is why I encourage you to pray the prayer of promise.

A prayer of promise is simply a prayer that incorporates Scripture into it. When you weave God's promises into your prayers, powerful things happen. That's because the addition of God's Word gives greater weight to what you are saying. It also enlarges your faith and encourages you to believe for the answers to your prayers. Praying God's promises helps you to pray in line with God's will as well.

THE PRAYER OF PROMISE BUILDS CONFIDENCE

I once heard a gifted pastor named Jerry Cook describe how God views us. He said, "God views us through our future. We view ourselves from our past." We look at our failures and the way we are at this moment. God looks at us the way He made us to be. He sees the end result. God accepts us just as we are, but He isn't going to leave us that way. Because He loves us so much, He is going to help us become all He created us to be. If something in us needs to be changed, *He* changes us as we surrender ourselves to Him.

God's doesn't expect us to be perfect in *performance* but perfect in *heart*. We need to know that God *already* views us as perfect when He looks into our hearts and sees Jesus there. Failure to understand this can keep us forever striving for the unattainable and eventually giving up because we feel we can never be all we "should" be.

In our flesh we strive to succeed. We feel we're worth something when we win, worthless when we lose.

What we demand of ourselves is always limited by the outer layer. Human perfection can only be as good as that. But God says He wants to make you something more than your human excellence. You will rise to the

We do not stand strong in our power; we stand strong in God's power.

level and degree you sense His love in your life. When you look in the mirror and see the excellence of Jesus reflected back, that's when you will have a sense of your true worth.

Total wholeness and restoration was God's plan for your life from the beginning, and you are to live in confidence about that. He has said many wonderful things in His Word about you, and as you pray these promises you will be remembering the truth about yourself as you stand in *His* perfection.

7 Prayers

HERE ARE SEVEN THINGS THAT GOD SAYS ARE ALWAYS TRUE ABOUT YOU. Praying these as a prayer of promise will build confidence in your heart:

I am a child of God, and my inheritance comes from Him.
But as many as received Him, to them He gave the right to become children of God. (John 1:12)

I have a special, God-ordained purpose.
Eye has not seen, nor ear heard, nor have entered into the heart of man the things which God has prepared for those who love Him. (1 Cor. 2:9)

I have been created with a specific calling.
Let each one remain with God in that calling in which he was called. (1 Cor. 7:24)

I am never alone.
I am with you always, even to the end of the age. (Matt. 28:20)

I am never forgotten.
God has not cast away His people whom He foreknew. (Rom. 11:2)

I am loved.
As the Father loved Me, I also have loved you. (John 15:9)

I am a winner.

In all these things we are more than conquerors
through Him who loved us. (Rom. 8:37)

When you pray, thank God for the good things He
says about you. It will help you to believe them!

THE PRAYER OF PROMISE BRINGS MATURITY

One of the last times I saw Mary Anne, my Christian
counselor, before she moved away, I went to her for
some problem that I don't even remember the details
of now. What I *do* remember was her wise counsel,
which amounted to two words: "Grow up," she said
lovingly.

"What?" I asked.

"It's time to grow up, Stormie," she repeated in her
patient voice. When my mother screamed those words
at me for years, it felt like a beating. When Mary Anne
said them, it felt like the Holy Spirit.

"Grow up?" I repeated, hoping she would give me
just a little more information.

"Yes, Stormie. You need to get alone with the Lord
and ask Him the questions you're asking me. . . ."

Everything she said felt right to me, and I laughed about it later when I told Michael. "You've got to admit that when you go to a counselor for help and she tells you to grow up, it's a sign of emotional health to see how funny that is."

Let the weak say, "I am strong."
JOEL 3:10

A point comes in our walk with the Lord when we've had enough teaching, enough counseling, enough deliverance, and enough knowledge of God's ways to be able to stand on our own two feet and say, "I am not going to live on the negative side of life any more." We can't depend on someone to hold our hand and make difficult times go away. We have to "grow up" and take responsibility for our lives. We have to decide we won't be the victims of our circumstances because God has given us a way out. We are not to stand in our own power but to stand strong in Him.

Standing strong in the Lord, we stand strong against the enemy. We don't cry, complain, and lament over what is not. We rejoice over what *is* and all that God is doing. We stand strong in what we know and in whom we trust. All of this happens when we pray and believe God's promises.

To pray the prayer of promise, you need to get clear in your mind the things that are always true about God and hold them alongside what is happening in your life to see if they line up. If you fear God is punishing you for something, does that line up with God's goodness? Don't focus on what's going on around you, but rather focus on what's in you.

HERE ARE SEVEN THINGS THAT ARE ALWAYS TRUE ABOUT GOD. These can become a prayer of promise for you.

> *I know God is a good God.*
> Good and upright is the LORD. (Ps. 25:8)
> *I know God is on my side.*
> The LORD is on my side. (Ps. 118:6)

I know God's laws and ways are for my benefit.

The judgments of the LORD are true and righteous
altogether . . . and in keeping them there is great
reward. (Ps. 19: 9, 11)

I know God is always with me.

I will never leave you nor forsake you. (Heb. 13:5)

I know God wants me restored.

You have delivered my soul from death. (Ps. 116:8)

I know God's promises to me will never fail.

Your faithfulness endures to all generations.
(Ps. 119:90)

I know God is always the winner.

He shall prevail against His enemies. (Is. 42:13)

THE PRAYER OF PROMISE RELEASES YOU TO LIVE IN GOD'S FULLNESS

There is a definite dividing line between God's kingdom and
Satan's, and there are people on the fringes of each. It doesn't
take much to put people over the edge into Satan's territory
and allow him to control a piece of their heart in the process.
All it takes is accepting a little lie like "It's my body," "It's my
life," or "I have my rights." Such lies lead to a little lust, a
little adultery, a little stealing, and a little murder.

All evil happens by deception. The devil entices us to accept things that are in opposition to God's ways. He appeals to our flesh and clouds issues to make them appear various shades of gray. We accept the gray as just a different shade of white instead of the alteration of black it really is. You are either lined up with God's kingdom or with Satan's. Black is black and white is white.

The good news is: *We don't have to listen to lies.* We may think we must give serious credence to everything that comes into our minds, but we don't. We only have to examine our thoughts in the light of the Word of God and see if they line up properly.

An evil spirit is always behind deception. This means that every deception brings bondage, which can only be removed by replacing it with God's truth and living accordingly. Without God's Word filling your mind with truth, you can't identify the lies. And without daily praying, "Lord, keep me undeceived," you can't ward off the deceiver. Everything you don't know about God will be used against you by the devil.

One of the first steps of obedience is to take charge of your mind. Unless you allow the truth of God's Word to fill and rule your mind, the deceiver creeps in to manipulate you for his purpose. God wants us to be free of the death grip of sin, whether we've acted in ignorance or with full knowledge and whether we feel guilty or not. When you find you've been deceived, immediately confess and repent. Ask God to pour His mercy upon you and release you from the death penalty of your sin.

After you confess and pray, don't let the devil continue to accuse you. You have cleaned the slate with God, so be released to live in the fullness of all God has for you.

THE PRAYER OF PROMISE BRINGS PROVISION IN JESUS' NAME

Imagine the power of Jesus' name for those who know and love Him. Certain guarantees and rewards are inherent in simply acknowledging the name of Jesus. For example the Bible says, "The name of the LORD is a strong tower; the righteous run into it and are safe" (Prov. 18:10). There is a covering of protection over anyone who turns to the name of the Lord.

The Lord has many names in the Bible, and each one expresses an aspect of His nature or one of His attributes. When we acknowledge Him by those names, we invite Him to be those things to us. For example, He is called Healer. When we say "Jesus, You are my Healer" and mix it with faith, it brings this attribute to bear upon our lives. This is praying a prayer of promise.

One of the reasons we do not have the wholeness, fulfillment, and peace we desire is that we have not acknowledge God as the answer to our every need. We think, "He may have given me eternal life, but I don't know if He can handle my financial problems." Or we think, "I know He can lead me to a better job, but I'm not sure if He can mend this marriage." "He healed my back, but I don't know if He can take away my depression." The truth is He is *everything* we need, and we have to remember that always. In fact, it's good to tell yourself daily, "God is everything I need," and then say the name of the Lord that answers your specific need at that moment.

Do you need hope? He is called our Hope. Say, "Jesus, You are my Hope."

Are you weak? He is called our Strength. Say, "Jesus, You are my Strength."

Do you need advice? He is called Counselor. Say, "Jesus, You are my Counselor."

Do you feel oppressed? He is called Deliverer.

Are you lonely? He is called Companion and Friend.

He is also called Emmanuel, which means God with us. He is not some distant, cold being with no interest in you. He is Emmanuel, the God who is with you right now to the degree you acknowledge Him in your life.

HERE ARE SEVEN ATTRIBUTES OF THE LORD. Praying these as a prayer of promise will remind you that God knows and cares about you:

He is my Restorer. (Ps. 23:3)

He is my Comforter. (John 14:16)

He is my Strength. (Isa. 12:2)

He is my Hope. (Ps. 71:5)

He is my Resting Place. (Jer. 50:6)

He is my Fortress. (Ps. 18:2)

He is my Refuge from the Storm. (Isa. 25:4)

God is the supreme intellect who created us and knows us better than we will ever know ourselves. He is powerful on our behalf and loves us to the fullest possible measure. Without Him, complete healing won't happen in our lives. All the things that need to be worked in us will never come about. Acknowledging Him as the answer to every need is the very foundation upon which wholeness is built.

Our help is in the name of the LORD.

PSALM 124:8

The Prayer of

Blessing

The blessing of the LORD be upon you.

—PSALM 129:8

Prayer of Conf

The Prayer

r of Release

ayer of Submission

The Pray

Prayer of Promise

The Prayer of C

The Pra

Prayer of Prai

THE

Prayer

OF BLESSING

ONE YEAR I GAVE my six-year-old daughter, Amanda, a small decorative box. Inside it I put a small piece of jewelry that she had been wanting for a long time.

When she unwrapped the gift and saw the box, she happily remarked on every detail. "Oh Mommy, this is so beautiful! Look at the pink roses and the painted ribbons, and see how tiny the gold lock is. This is the prettiest box I've ever seen!"

She was about to put the box away in her room when I said, "Amanda, open it up."

She opened it and squealed, "Oh, thank you, Mommy! This is the necklace I wanted!" as she ran to a mirror to put it on.

I sat there thinking, *She would have been happy with just the pretty box.* And then I thought of how our heavenly Father gives us gifts, and often we don't unwrap them or possess all He has for us because we don't see them or we don't realize they are there for us or we don't ask for them. We let His gifts sit unopened.

THE PRAYER OF BLESSING FOR GOD'S POWER

God's power is a gift for us to use, among other things, for the healing of our souls, and anyone wanting emotional health and restoration must have access to it. God wants you to know the "exceeding greatness of His power toward us who believe" (Eph. 1:19), so He can "strengthen you with power through his Spirit in your inner being" (Eph. 3:16 NIV).

You can't conjure it up, take it by force, or demand God's power; you can only pray for it and receive it from Him. Oswald Chambers says that God's purpose for me is "that I depend on Him and His power now." By depending on God's power instead of your own, you are fulfilling God's purpose for your life.

If you feel powerless and weak in the face of your circumstances, then thank God that even though *you* are weak, *He* is not. He says, "My strength is made perfect in weakness" (2 Cor. 12:9). Just as Jesus was crucified in weakness and lives in all power now, the same is true for us if we come to Him in weakness. Our power comes from the Holy Spirit working in us. Jesus told His disciples, "You shall receive power when the Holy Spirit has come upon you" (Acts 1:8).

We are always in need of a fresh flow of the Holy Spirit. Ask for one daily. Every morning say, "God, I need a fresh flow of Your Holy Spirit power working in me this day. I am weak, but You are all-powerful. Be strong in me this day." This is a power-full prayer of blessing.

Don't be a victim of your circumstances. Don't allow yourself to be tormented. Don't sit back when life seems to be falling apart. Don't live your life in terms of human energy. Ask God for His power to move in your life, and let His power enable you to rise above your limitations.

If you ever become overwhelmed by how much you think you have to do to arrive at complete wholeness, or if you have doubts about whether you can actually do all that's required, then *you need to remind yourself that the Holy Spirit accomplishes wholeness in you, as you allow Him.* Let *Him* do it. All *you* have to do is tell God that you want *His* ways to become your ways, and then take one step at a time as each one is is revealed to you. God's power working in and through you will open up doors you never dreamed possible.

What good is God's power to you if you never receive and use it? Tell God you want to receive His gift of power and see how He blesses you with it. Your life depends on it.

THE PRAYER OF BLESSING FOR FAITH

Faith is a spiritual muscle that needs to be exercised in order to prevent atrophy, which makes our entire spiritual being weak. Faith is first a decision, then an exercise in obedience, than a gift from God as it is multiplied. Our first step of faith is taken when we decide we will receive Jesus as our Savior. After that, every time we decide to trust the Lord for anything, we build that faith. Whenever we decide not to trust God, we tear it down. Faith is our daily decision to trust God.

Faith is a gift from God in that He *enables* us to believe, but we have to obey by building on that faith. How do we start building faith? The first step is to be totally open and honest about any doubt in God's ability or His faithfulness to provide for our every need. Doubt emanates from a lie of the enemy, which says God is not all-powerful. If you've listened to this lie, confess it as sin.

The next step is to fill your mind with the Word: "Faith comes from hearing the message, and the message is heard through the word of Christ" (Rom. 10:17 NIV). Reading the Word daily, regularly submitting to Bible teaching, and speaking the Word aloud will build trust. Your mouth and heart have to be united in this.

Because your prayers will only be as strong as your faith in God, it's always good to read the Word before you pray. Ask God to give you faith every time you do and try to keep reading until you sense faith rising in your heart. Faith leads the way to answered prayer. Whenever I'm afraid or doubt that my life is secure,

I read the Bible until I sense God's peace in me. The more I read, the more hope I have. Then, when I pray, I'm confident that God will answer my prayers.

The Bible says of the people who could not go into the Promised Land, "They could not enter in because of unbelief" (Heb. 3:19). Don't let that happen to you. Choose to enter into all that God has for you by

> *Faith is unutterable trust in God, trust that never dreams He would not stand by us.* OSWALD CHAMBERS

praying the prayer of blessing for faith. When it has blossomed, faith gives birth to hope. Hope and faith together give you a vision for your life.

THE PRAYER OF BLESSING FOR WHOLENESS

God created the world by speaking it into existence. Since we are made in His likeness and His Spirit dwells in us, we have the power to speak our own worlds into existence too. When we speak negatively about ourselves or our circumstances, we cut off the possibility of things being any different.

Early in my walk with the Lord I spoke many negatives like "I'm a failure." "I'm ugly." "Nothing ever goes right." "Nobody really cares about me," until one day the Holy Spirit spoke to my heart through Proverbs 18:21: "Death and life are in the power of the tongue." A quick inventory of the things I had said aloud and in my mind revealed that I had been speaking words of death and not life. This thought was frightening.

One clear example of what this Scripture was saying to me had to do with my speech problems. I'd had them since childhood and was teased about them all through school. As soon as I was old enough to work and afford professional help, I worked with a speech therapist every week. I practiced day after day, year after year, to gain what seemed to be only a little improvement.

Two years after Michael and I were married, we did a few music concerts together, and I was asked to speak on health care in weekly classes at church. In spite of all my hard work with the therapist, I still lost my voice about halfway through each engagement due to the tension in my neck. I became deeply discouraged and felt like a failure.

"I'll never be able to speak right," I cried time and again in despair and frustration. But as I spoke those words one day, the Lord spoke to my heart saying, *"You're bringing death to your situation because you're not speaking the truth about it.*

"What does that mean, Lord? Am I supposed to deny what's really happening to me?" I asked God.

Do not speak what you think to be truth or what seems to be truth, He replied to my heart, *but rather speak what you know to be the truth of my Word.*

Over the next few days, certain Scriptures came to my attention. Isaiah 32:4: "The stammering tongue will be fluent and clear" (NIV), and "I have put My words in your mouth" (Isa. 51:16).

After that, each time I was tempted to give in to discouragement, I spoke those Scriptures to myself and said, "Thank You, Lord, for helping me to speak slowly and clearly. I can do all things through Christ who strengthens me. Praise You, Lord that You will give me the words to say and anoint them to have life."

I purposely cleared out other negatives from my speech. I no longer said "I'm a failure" because God's Word says the opposite is true about me. I stopped saying "I'm hopeless" and started acknowledging God as the hope of my life.

Soon after, when I was asked to speak at a large women's meeting, I took all my fears about it to the Lord in prayer and didn't let my mouth say that I was

When talking about yourself, speak words of hope, health, encouragement, life, and purpose—they are God's truth for you.

going to fail. I spoke God's truth instead of voicing my own negative opinions. As a result, my talk went so well that an entire speaking ministry opened up to me.

We often speak what we hear the devil saying to our minds or we repeat to ourselves what someone else said to us years ago "You're worthless. You'll never amount to anything." The Bible says, "You are snared by the words of your mouth" (Prov. 6:2). That includes our silent messages to ourselves as well as what we speak aloud.

When talking about yourself, speak words of hope, health, encouragement, life, and purpose—they are God's truth for you. Wipe words of hopelessness, doubt, and negativity from your vocabulary. What you speak may seem harmless to you, but it affects your body and soul. It promotes either health and life or sickness and death. Walk in obedience to the Lord by only speaking words that reflect the wholeness you desire.

God has so much for you. Learn to pray His way so He can overflow you with His blessings beyond what you can imagine.

The eyes of the LORD are on the righteous, and His ears are open to their prayers.

— 1 PETER 3:12

acknowledgments

Grateful acknowledgment is made to the following publishers for permission to reprint this copyrighted material. All copyrights are held by the author.

Omartian, Stormie. *Finding Peace for Your Heart* (Nashville: Thomas Nelson Publishers, 1991).

Omartian, Stormie. *Lord, I Want to Be Whole* (Nashville: Thomas Nelson Publishers, 2000).

Omartian, Stormie. *Praying God's Will for Your Life,* (Nashville: Thomas Nelson Publishers, 2001).

Omartian, Stormie. *Praying God's Will for Your Life Workbook and Journal* (Nashville: Thomas Nelson Publishers, 2002).